Discard
NHCPL

EARTH-FRIENDLY DESIGN

ANNE WELSBACHER

The text of this book is printed on Lustro Offset Environmental paper, which is made with **30 percent recycled post-consumer waste fibers**. Using paper with post-consumer waste fibers helps to protect endangered forests, conserve mature trees, keep used paper out of landfills, save energy in the manufacturing process, and reduce greenhouse gas emissions. The remaining fiber comes from forestlands that are managed in a socially and environmentally responsible way, as certified by independent organizations. Also, the mills that manufactured this paper purchased certified renewable energy, such as solar or wind energy, to cover its production.

Lerner Publications Company
A division of Lerner Publishing Group, Inc.
241 First Avenue North
Minneapolis, MN 55401 U.S.A.

Website address: www.lernerbooks.com

Library of Congress Cataloging-in-Publication Data

Welsbacher, Anne 1955-
Earth-friendly design / by Anne Welsbacher.
p. cm. — (Saving our living earth)
Includes bibliographical references and index.
ISBN 978-0-8225-7564-1 (lib. bdg. : alk. paper)
1. Design, Industrial—Environmental aspects—Juvenile literature. 2. Green products—Design—Juvenile literature. 3. Green technology—Juvenile literature. I. Title.
TS171.4W44 2009
745.2—dc22 2007035925

Manufactured in the United States of America
1 2 3 4 5 6 — DP — 14 13 12 11 10 09

CONTENTS

INTRODUCTION

As campers on planet Earth, we make mistakes. We dump waste into our water. We use things for a short time and then throw them away. We cut down forests to build homes. We dig up the ground to get fuel to cool, warm, and light our homes. We drive vehicles that also need fuel dug from the ground. What have all these mistakes done to our planet?

Chemicals from waste products pollute the water and soil. Polluted land cannot support growth. Air and water polluted from our machines increase disease in animals and plants. Some are dying and even becoming extinct.

A cloud of thick smog hangs over downtown Los Angeles, California. The state of California has adopted many new laws to control air pollution, especially pollution caused by vehicles.

All life is interdependent. We depend on one another for healthy life. The loss of even some animals and plants can hurt us all and the planet itself. For example, trees process certain chemicals, helping to clean the air. When large tracts of forests are cut down, we lose their pollution-fighting work.

Air pollution can also cause Earth's air temperature to rise. This process is called global warming. Global warming changes wind patterns. This can alter weather, the kinds of storms we have, how oceans move, and more.

We can help our planet heal. One important way to do this is to change how we make and use cars, houses, buildings, and other things.

We can make machines so that they do not pollute the air, water, or land. We can design cars so that they do not need fuels dug from the ground. We can build houses that do not need wood cut from trees in forests. We can buy products that are made from renewable or recycled materials.

These actions are part of a concept called Earth-friendly, or green, design. The best part about Earth-friendly design is that anybody anywhere can use it to help the planet—including you.

The best part about Earth-Friendly design is that anybody anywhere can use it to help the planet.

EARTH-FRIENDLY DESIGN

When your grandparents were kids, they had no cell phones, computers, DVD players, or digital games. The average house then was half the size of a modern house. There was only one TV in the house, and its screen was smaller too.

Your great-great-grandparents watched no TV at all. They had no microwave ovens or modern refrigerators. Their families most likely did not have a car. If they did, the whole family shared one car.

Your ancestors sewed much of their own clothing. They also mended torn clothes or resewed them to fit when the kids grew and needed larger sizes. There were no shopping malls and far fewer clothing stores.

We take our possessions and many other things for granted. Manufactured products make life easier, and they can be fun to use. But they come at a cost to all living things.

MORE, MORE, MORE

Sometimes our computers, cell phones, and other things break. Sometimes we want new ones. We throw away the old ones. They end up in landfills. Landfills are taking up space needed for living and growing. Chemicals inside of discarded products leach into the ground. The chemicals poison our water and land.

Facing page: A family in the 1950s gathers around the television. After World War II, people began using more electricity to power hot water heaters, large refrigerators, and televisions. *This page:* Many of the things that we throw away end up in landfills.

The Trans-Alaska pipeline carries oil from the Arctic Ocean to southern Alaska. Part of the pipeline was built aboveground so that the oil would not melt permafrost on the tundra.

Our homes are bigger than they once were. More lumber is needed to build them. The wood for that lumber comes from forests. But new trees cannot grow fast enough to replace the trees that are cut down. Half of the world's forests are gone. Home and building construction creates much of that loss.

Our cars run on gasoline. Gasoline is made from oil. Oil, coal, and natural gas are fossil fuels. We dig these fuels from the ground. To get to them, land must be cleared. Roads must be made and big holes dug. Pipelines, power lines, and other equipment must be brought in. Factories, also called plants, must be built to process the fuels taken from the ground.

FOSSIL FUELS

Fossil fuels were formed from dead plants and animals. They took millions of years to form. Fossil fuels are nonrenewable sources of energy. This means that once they run out, they are gone forever.

This entire process destroys the land and other resources where the digging takes place. It kills and drives away wildlife that needs the land to survive.

FUELS AND AIR

Our computers and other appliances use electricity, another source of energy. Unlike fossil fuels, electricity is not dug from the ground. But electricity is created by plants that burn fossil fuels.

Burning fossil fuels releases gases and pollutants into the air. One kind of air pollution caused by burning fossil fuels is called smog. Among the many types of pollutants are nitrogen oxides, carbon dioxides, and carbon monoxides.

Pollutants are toxic, or poisonous. They make us sick. Some can cause cancer. They worsen illnesses such as asthma and heart disease. They damage our lungs.

Some pollutants like carbon dioxide also stay in Earth's atmosphere. They hold the sun's heat near Earth the same way that windows trap heat inside a greenhouse. This greenhouse effect heats up our air and causes global warming.

Global warming has brought changes all over the planet. Some places have suffered from lack of rain, or drought. In places that typically receive a lot of snow every year, snowfall has decreased. This upsets the growing season for plants and wildlife that rely on snowmelt for their water.

In other places, heat spells have been hotter and lasted much longer than usual. They have killed people and wildlife. The warmer

A girl with asthma uses an inhaler to help her breathe. Air pollution can bring on asthma symptoms.

temperatures are melting the oceans' polar ice caps. This melted ice raises the water level in the oceans. The water is flooding areas close to the shore.

GREEN DESIGN

Earth-friendly design allows us to make things and to use resources in a way that protects the planet. Using green design principles, or ideas, we build houses with materials that are plentiful. For example, we use existing wood saved from buildings that were taken apart, instead of new wood made from trees that were cut down.

We heat our homes in ways that use fewer or no fossil fuels. We install better insulation. Insulation is a material that keeps cold or warm air from coming inside. This means that less energy is needed to heat or cool the building. We also build windows with extra panes. They fit so tightly that no cold (or hot) air can come in around the edges.

We design cars that do not need to use as much gasoline. For example, we create new systems to run our cars. The systems run on both batteries and fuel so that our cars do not need to use as much fuel. We explore other kinds of fuels that do not pollute the air and that can be renewed. For example, we develop fuels from grains or grasses that can be grown easily.

We build things out of strong, quality materials so that they last longer. These items do not have to be replaced as often. This reduces the amount of waste we create. We remove dangerous chemicals in our computers, cell phones, and other electronic items before we throw them away.

Earth-friendly design is a way of doing things that helps to change how we use and affect the planet.

Biking instead of driving is one way to help the environment. Bicycles do not pollute the air because they do not burn fossil fuels.

OUR WEB OF LIFE

Earth-friendly design is about more than building things. Everything we do affects the land, air, and other living creatures. How we eat, play, work, sleep, and live can help or hurt the planet just as much as how we build our houses or drive our cars.

Using principles of green design, we can decide to live closer to where we work and go to school. We can buy things made from nontoxic materials. We can buy fewer things and recycle the things we no longer want. We can live closer to our neighbors and share items that we don't use frequently.

Perhaps most important, we can learn more. We can learn how the ways we live our lives affect people everywhere. How we make things, move them, use them, reuse them, and dispose of them affects us all. Earth-friendly design can help us make our planet healthier.

CHAPTER TWO

GREEN VEHICLES

The single most polluting action most people can take is to drive a car. Cars, trucks, and buses create almost 20 percent of the United States' pollution. Vehicles burn gasoline to run, which emits, or releases, many kinds of pollutants into the air.

Tailpipe emissions are the main source of ground-level ozone. Ozone is a form of oxygen that can be harmful when trapped in large amounts near the ground. Ground-level ozone is a part of smog.

The single most polluting action most people take is to drive a car.

Auto emissions also release carbon dioxide into the air. The more gas a car uses, the more carbon dioxide it releases into the air. Carbon dioxide traps heat near Earth, which causes global warming.

Gasoline is made from oil. If we continue to use as much oil and other fossil fuels as we currently do, nobody knows how many years they will last. But many experts guess that oil will be used up by about 2050.

Green vehicles are designed to burn less gas. They also are designed to use fuels other than gas, or alternative fuels. Burning less gas means that fewer pollutants are released into the air. It also means that we will not need to depend on nonrenewable sources of energy.

The exhaust that comes out of the tailpipe of a car includes emissions of nitrous oxide and particles of soot from gasoline or diesel.

HYBRID CARS

Many people own mixed-breed dogs. Perhaps a dog's mother is a Labrador retriever and its father is a German shepherd. The dog is a hybrid—a mix of breeds.

Many green-design cars also mix different "breeds." During parts of their driving time, they burn gas. But during other parts of the drive, they use electricity or batteries instead. Because they use two different sources of power, they are called hybrid cars.

When a driver turns on a car and moves the car from stop to go, it takes a lot of energy to get the car moving. In most cars, gas-burning engines provide this heavy-duty power needed to get the car started.

Once the car is moving along, it does not need all that energy to keep going. When the driver stops at red lights, the car does not need any energy at all—it is sitting still. But older cars burn gas whether moving or sitting. This wastes gas and adds to air pollution.

A hybrid car, such as the Toyota Prius, has an engine that runs on gasoline. But the hybrid also has an electric motor that is run by a battery. The electric motor starts the car. Both the electric motor and gas-powered engine supply energy to speed up, or accelerate, the car. When the car waits at a stoplight, the gas engine stops and no gas is burned.

Hybrid cars also recapture energy that would be lost in older cars. When a driver steps on the brakes, energy is released as

CITY DRIVING

How far a vehicle can travel using a gallon (4 liters) of fuel is called fuel economy. Vehicles usually get better fuel economy when driving on the highway. That's because there's less stopping and sitting. Cars with good fuel economy burn less gasoline and create less air pollution.

The newest models of the Toyota Prius can get about 46 miles per gallon (20 kilometers per liter) or more. That's nearly two times as far as a medium-sized car could go.

friction from the metal brakes rubbing together. The hybrid car takes back that energy and uses it to recharge the battery.

DIESEL FUEL

Another form of fuel made from oil is diesel. Diesel fuel is more efficient, or less wasteful, than gasoline. About 3 to 4 gallons (11 to 15 liters) of diesel provide the same amount of energy as 5 gallons (19 liters) of gas.

But diesel is dirty. When it is burned to produce energy, it emits far more pollution into the air than burning gas does. Diesel burns at lower temperatures. This causes it to produce more uncombusted carbons—carbons that don't burn up in the heat. These carbons create more soot.

Almost all trucks and school buses use diesel fuel. Finding a way to make diesel less dirty would help lower the pollution these vehicles are causing. Also, if diesel

BUS FUMES

Diesel buses belch a plume of black, stinky smoke when they start and stop. That exhaust is unhealthy to breathe. Diesel exhaust goes inside a bus as well. In fact, exhaust levels can be even higher inside a bus than outside, especially in the back if the windows are closed.

could be cleaner, more cars could be designed to burn it. Then more fuel would be saved because less would need to be burned.

Engineers are working to make diesel cleaner. In 2006 a new kind of diesel was developed that is 97 percent cleaner than the old diesel. It contains less sulfur, an element that pollutes the air. This cleaner fuel reduces by 10 percent the amount of soot emissions from trucks and other vehicles using diesel. It also will work with new engines to reduce pollution even more—as much as 95 percent.

BIOFUELS AND BIODIESELS

Improvements in vehicle design and cleaner diesel fuels are helping to reduce our use of fossil fuels and lower the amount of pollutants we put into the air. But they are short-term solutions to the energy problems we face. They still rely on limited resources and pollute the air.

Another approach is to use biofuels in our vehicles instead of fossil fuels. Biofuels are not made from fossil fuels. Biofuels are made from organic materials, meaning they came from living things.

Biofuels can be developed from crops such as corn and soybeans, food crops that farmers grow. These crops are easy to grow and harvest, and they can be replaced every growing season.

Biofuels help farmers earn more income as well. Biofuels provide a new market

Molly Harrall fills up her family's car in England with biodiesel. Diesel cars are common in many parts of Europe.

for farming. Biofuels also can be made from grasses such as switchgrass or even from waste such as animal manure.

Biofuels are still being developed. Most are limited in use. They can be used to create electricity. But few current vehicles are designed to process biofuels.

Biodiesels already are in use. The European Union has led the way in biodiesel production. In the United States, more than 150 biodiesel plants have been built. These plants process soybeans and other crops into fuels that can be used like diesel in vehicles.

GREEN DESIGN DECISIONS

Some carmakers, such as Honda and Toyota, are designing hybrid cars. Other companies, such as Volkswagen and Mercedes-Benz, are designing their cars to work with biodiesels.

Other design approaches lower fuel use too. For example, a car's shape can reduce the force of air pressing against the car as it moves. This is called aerodynamic design. Also, vehicles designed with lightweight materials and smaller engines usually need less fuel than do heavy, high-powered vehicles.

All of these approaches have drawbacks. Designing and building new cars and vehicle systems takes time and costs money. And customers do not always want to buy or drive these new vehicles, especially if they have to change the way they drive.

For example, the amount of gas used in a hybrid car depends on how the car is driven. A driver must follow guidelines to control how much energy is created, or wasted. Using the brakes at certain times and speeding up at certain times determine energy use. If a driver does not carefully follow these guidelines, the hybrid car uses much more gas—nearly as much as a traditional type of car.

Some buyers would rather use diesel vehicles. But in the United States, it is easier for drivers to find stations that sell conventional gasoline than it is to find stations that offer clean diesel, biodiesels, or biofuels. And sometimes fuel labeled "biodiesel" is actually only a blend of a small amount of biofuel with a large amount of old diesel fuel. It is only slightly less polluting than the old fuel.

Even if more cars were designed to use biodiesels and biofuels, farmers might not be able to produce enough crops to create the amount of fuel that would be needed. The extra labor and land needed to grow crops for biofuels would make it harder to grow other crops, such as wheat, for food. Food would become very expensive. And

Machines that burn fossil fuels are often used to harvest biofuel crops, such as corn.

This city bus uses hybrid technology to run. In addition to reducing pollution, hybrid buses can save city governments money on the cost of fuel.

growing, harvesting, and processing biofuels can create additional pollution.

Although many of these approaches reduce our need for fossil fuels, they do not solve our environmental problems. We can further reduce pollution by using mass transit whenever possible. Most trains and buses still run on electricity and fossil fuels. But they carry many people instead of just a few. This means less fuel per person is used. We also can travel using our own renewable energy: we can walk or ride a bike.

CAR SHARE

Car sharing services are popping up in crowded cities. Members pay monthly fees to use a car when and where needed. When finished driving, members simply leave the cars in a special zone. Their monthly rates cover insurance, fuel, and car repairs. Sharing cars means fewer cars are on the road. As a result, less fuel is burned and less pollution ends up in the air.

EARTH-FRIENDLY PRODUCTS

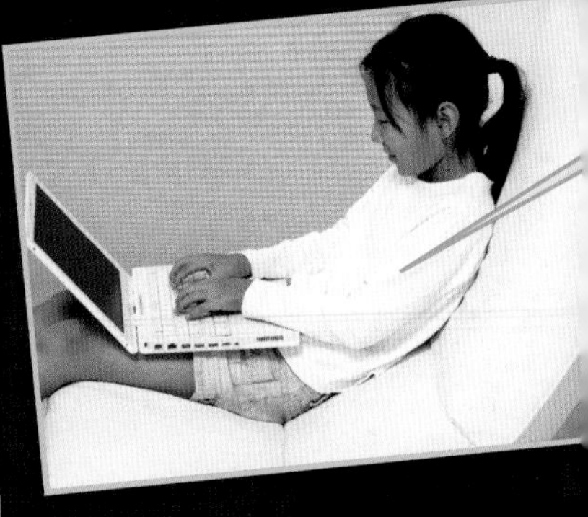

Do you have a cell phone? Does it take pictures? Does it play a tune you downloaded from your computer?

Your parents or older sibling probably had a phone that couldn't take pictures or play new tunes. They could only use their phones to call people. New cell phones have new gadgets. They are more fun, easier to use, and more colorful. We buy the new phones. But what do we do with our old ones?

Do you use a computer? Computers keep getting smaller and faster. People buy new ones, sometimes every two or three years. But what do we do with our old computers?

LIFE CYCLES OF THINGS

All things that people make go through a life cycle. First, materials are gathered. Metals such as mercury and cadmium are dug from the ground. Oil is drilled. Lumber is cut.

Trucks, trains, and other vehicles carry the materials to plants and factories. Then they are processed or put together into products. Plastic is made and molded. Sometimes chemicals are used to make the products.

Then the finished products are distributed. Special boxes are made to hold them. Packing materials are wrapped around them to keep them from breaking. Trucks and trains carry the finished products to stores and warehouses.

People buy the products and use them. The items are fueled with electricity or batteries. When the items break, people get them repaired or throw them away.

Left: A girl uses a laptop computer. *Background image:* Many old phones and computers remain in people's homes. Unused electronics should be recycled, donated, or returned to the company that made them.

THE LIFE CYCLE OF PRODUCTS

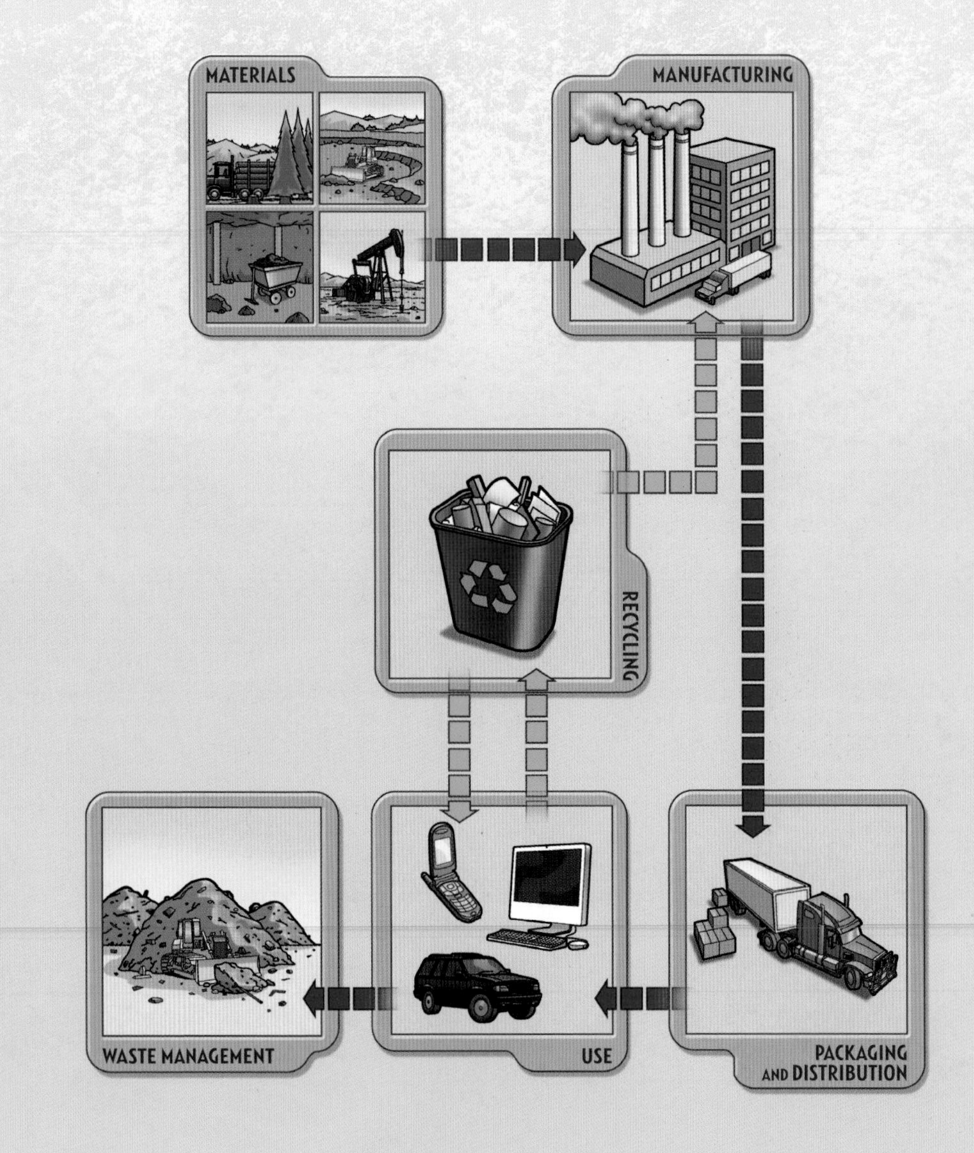

Every stage in the life cycle of a product uses materials and energy and creates some waste and pollution.

A truck brings lumber up a mountain road. Where will the lumber end up?

BROKEN CYCLES

Each step in a product's life cycle involves processes that damage our planet, our health, or both. To dig into the ground, we must bring in equipment, build roads, and cut down trees and other plant life. The equipment uses gas, oil, and other nonrenewable fuels. These fuels pollute the air and water. The vehicles that carry the products also use these fuels.

The chemicals used to build some products can be unhealthy for the people building them. Some substances can also be unhealthy for people who use the products.

For example, lead is used in TV and computer monitors. Lead protects people from dangerous X-rays. But it is very hazardous to people's health. If lead gets into the body, it can damage organs. It can weaken bones and the blood's ability to make red blood cells.

The materials used for packaging include paper made from trees. Forests of trees are cut down to make paper. Other packing materials, such as plastic, are

Make a difference in the use stage of a product's life. Turn off computers when you're not using them.

made of elements that are not biodegradable. This means that they will not break down, or decay, after they are thrown away.

Electronic items, especially computers, use a lot of energy. More than half of the energy that goes into a computer is wasted. For example, the energy used by the computer to keep it running makes it very hot. A fan inside the computer uses energy to keep it from getting too hot to touch. This wasted energy has nothing to do with the reasons we use a computer.

People often leave electronics running, even when they are not using them. This wastes more energy. The electricity used to run these electronics is made from burning coal, oil, and gas. Burning these fossil fuels emits pollutants into the air.

Even throwing away things pollutes Earth. Trucks that burn fossil fuels haul the waste to landfills and recycling centers.

Electronic waste, or e-waste, can be especially dangerous to the health of living things. Inside televisions, computers, and cell phones are toxic materials, including lead, mercury, and other substances. When a TV, computer, or cell phone goes into a landfill, these materials can leak into the soil and water.

Sometimes, waste is put into an incinerator and burned. The plastic in electronic items releases toxins when it is burned.

EARTH-FRIENDLY ELECTRONICS

New design ideas are changing the life cycle of things. Green engineering affects each stage in the cycle of electronics. Some companies, including Sony, Panasonic, Apple, and Hewlett-Packard, are replacing the lead in their monitors. They are using a compound made of tin, silver, and copper, instead of lead.

In Europe the Restriction of Hazardous Substances (RoHS) Directive bans the use of certain dangerous materials in electronic products. China also has banned certain substances from electronics manufacturing.

Plastic is made from petroleum, which comes from oil. Oil is a nonrenewable resource. Also, petroleum-based plastic is not biodegradable. It will not decay.

Some companies are exploring ways to stop using petroleum-based plastic. They are making "plastics" from biomass products. Biomass products are made from plants and organic waste that are biodegradable.

OOPS!

Sometimes a good idea needs more work.

Biopolymers are substances that will break down safely into the soil when thrown away. But they do not work well on products that get hot. One company's scientist created a printer with a biopolymer covering. On a hot day, he put the printer in the trunk of his car and drove to a meeting to show off his invention. When he arrived, the printer's cover had melted.

Back to the drawing board. The company found chemicals that help keep corn-based plastic from melting. The company also placed the plastic only on computer parts that do not get too hot, such as monitors.

This green restaurant in Boston encourages its customers to compost and recycle their trash. The restaurant serves locally grown food on biodegradable dishware.

Companies make covers for cell phones from these biomass materials. Unlike plastic, these covers will safely break down after they are thrown away. And biomass materials can be easily renewed.

Some companies, such as Toshiba, offer computers that can be upgraded. Instead of throwing away your computer, you can add new features onto the one you have.

In early 2006, Nokia began using less packaging materials to ship cell phones. The new packages use 54 percent less material and are thinner. About five thousand fewer trucks per year are used for shipping.

Other household appliances are becoming more energy efficient. New refrigerators and freezers use up to 75 percent less energy than older models.

In the United States, a labeling system called Energy Star identifies the most efficient appliances to make it easier for people to find and buy them. Other countries, such as Australia and the United Kingdom, have their own standards and labels for energy efficiency.

ELECTRONICS: ALREADY GREEN?

In some ways, electronics are already green. For example, people can shop on the Internet. Then they do not have to drive to the store. Instead, trucks bring the products to their homes. Trucks can cause pollution. But delivery trucks carry many different items to many different households in just one trip. This saves gas and reduces pollution.

PAPER

The magazines and books we read are made of paper, which comes from trees that are cut down. Large amounts of paper are used to make these products.

Imagine a space that is 64,000 cubic feet (1,800 cubic meters)—a square that is 40 feet (12 m) long, 40 feet wide, and 40 feet high. Fill that space with paper, and you have 1 ton (0.9 metric ton) of paper. The publisher Random House buys 120,000 tons (108,862 metric tons) of paper every year to print its books.

Many publishers use recycled paper for some of their paper needs. But they use only a small amount—about 5 percent. If publishers use recycled paper for 30 percent of their paper, they could save more than 4 million trees. They could reduce greenhouse gases by more than 500 million pounds (227 million kilograms) every year.

Standard ink is made from petroleum products. Many publishers are turning to ink made from soybeans, a renewable resource.

Some publishers are also taking carbon-neutral steps. This means that they are trying to make up for the pollution they produce. For example, for every dollar a

A worker puts a new roll of paper on the press at St Ives Printing in Cleveland, Ohio. The company uses paper that is approved by the Forest Stewardship Council (FSC). This means the trees used to make the paper were harvested in Earth-friendly ways.

publisher spends on petroleum products, it might donate a dollar to a company that makes renewable energy.

OTHER PRODUCTS

Companies that make and sell many other products are also increasing their efforts to improve the life cycles of goods. The European Union encourages product makers to use certain green rules throughout a product's life cycle. If they do, their product is given an EU Eco-label. The label is a drawing of a flower. This makes it easier for customers to know which products are more Earth friendly than others.

For example, to earn an eco-label flower, shoes must be made in a way that avoids polluting water and air. They are sold in recycled packaging. Bedding, vacuum cleaners, clothing, cleaning and gardening products, and many other items have received eco-labels.

Earth-friendly furniture can be made from the wood in old furniture, houses, or other things that have been disassembled. Factories also discard some wood after building projects. The Rainforest Alliance awards green products a "rediscovered wood certification" label.

Bamboo plants provide a strong, plentiful building material for many household items, from furniture to window shades. Bamboo grows fast. Growers often do not use pesticides to grow it.

Recycled plastics and metals also can be used to build furniture and other products. The Icon Chair, from Emeco, is made from 80 percent recycled aluminum.

A new plan by Wal-Mart orders the company's sixty thousand suppliers to reduce packaging by 5 percent. This will save more than 716,500 tons (650,000 metric tons) of carbon dioxide emissions.

This bench is made from 100 percent recycled plastic, or Plaswood. This material looks like wood but is much more durable.

BUILDINGS AND HOUSES

How people make and live in buildings affects the environment. What kinds of materials do we use? Do they harm our health? How do we carry them to the site of the building? What happens to them after we tear down the buildings? These are factors in green design.

BUILDING MATERIALS

The lumber used to build many structures comes from trees. Just as people and other animals breathe oxygen, trees "breathe," or process, carbon dioxide. Too much carbon dioxide in the air leads to global warming. Trees help reduce the amount of carbon dioxide in the air. They help reduce global warming.

After trees are cut down for wood, the wood must be carried to the site of the building. Roads are built into the forest to carry the wood. Building the roads destroys land and displaces the wildlife that lives on it. Trucks that drive on the roads and carry the wood emit pollutants into the air.

Many buildings using green design are built with recycled wood. This wood was already used for something else.

Green buildings also are built from local, or nearby, resources. Local materials do not need to be carried long distances by truck. This cuts down on air pollutant emissions.

Imagine a space covered by about ten houses. Then imagine that space filled with trees. That is the amount of forest cut down to build just one large house.

ENERGY AND WATER

Green design principles also help to lower the amount of energy needed to heat and cool buildings. New windows and walls are better insulated. Less hot air enters in the summer, and less cold air seeps inside in the winter. Smaller houses save resources too. They need less energy to heat and cool them.

Roofs with solar panels, or tiles, can generate electricity for homes. These tiles convert sunlight into electricity. Most houses do not have roofs with solar tiles. But many soon will—even homes built with traditional lumber and designs.

Water, like trees, is a limited resource. How water in buildings is used and reused is also important in green design. Toilets can be made to use less water for flushing. Systems can be made to catch and use rainwater. Filters in plumbing systems can clean used water. The water then can be reused to water plants or to clean.

Solar tiles on the roofs of these Earth-friendly homes in Bristol, England, collect energy from the sun.

LEED

In 2000 the Leadership in Energy and Environmental Design, or LEED, rating system was created. LEED lists standards, or rules, for constructing buildings. The rules call for on-site work that does not harm the local environment. They also require that buildings save water, use energy efficiently, use green materials, and have a healthy indoor environment.

The standards are voluntary—they are not required by law. But they guide companies on how to build green. Any company that uses these rules can apply to have its buildings LEED certified.

Companies can market their buildings by saying that they used LEED standards to build them. People often want to rent or buy space in LEED-certified buildings because the costs to heat and cool them are low.

GREEN HOUSES

The first LEED standards were used in buildings where people work. Today builders and homeowners use these ideas for building new homes and redesigning or redecorating old homes.

The Hearst Tower in New York City was awarded top LEED certification. It was built with recycled aluminum and uses outdoor air to help cool the inside.

A couple in Oregon used old forest logs for the beams in their new house. But they did not cut down trees to get the logs. The logs had been cut and used long ago to build a barge.

This house has other green features too. A special entry area with two doors catches cold air and keeps it from going into the house. This means less fossil fuel is used to heat the home in the winter. And the house was placed to catch as much cool wind from the nearby mountains as it can. As a result, little electricity is needed to cool the house in warm summer months.

This Oregon house is one of the very first houses to be given LEED certification. Other houses in Oklahoma, Maine, and Michigan also are LEED certified. And thousands of homes in other states are being built or planned with LEED standards.

BUILDING GREEN CITIES

In 2006 Boston, Massachusetts, became the first U.S. city to require all buildings to meet certain LEED rating standards. Other cities—such as Washington, D.C.; New York City; and Pasadena, California—have added new laws requiring some LEED standards in building.

OLD MATERIALS, NEW HOUSES

Many homebuilders are turning back to materials people used long ago. Rammed-earth, adobe, and straw-bale houses are made of earth, mud, and even straw.

Houses made from these materials have many green elements. Often, building materials such as mud can be found right on the site. No trucks are needed to carry materials long distances. Many of these homes last a long time—longer than homes made of wood.

Even a properly made straw-bale house can last twice as long as a wooden

Straw-bale houses begin with wooden or steel frames. Bales are stacked within the frame. Straw makes good insulation and blocks most noises.

house. A straw-bale home is built with stacks of tightly tied bundles, or bales, which overlap one another like bricks. Stucco, plaster, cement, or other materials cover and protect the outer walls of the house.

Straw is a renewable resource. It grows easily and quickly. Using straw helps with another pollution problem too. Straw is what is left over after grain is processed for cattle and other animals to eat. Often that straw is burned, creating air pollution. So building from straw helps reduce the amount that is burned.

Rammed-earth houses are built by packing a mud mixture into wood or steel molds called formwork. The mixture must be a specific combination of sand and clay or cement. The mixture is compacted tightly and allowed to dry. Then more mud is added, compacted, and dried.

Rammed-earth walls look like stone when finished.

This process creates walls that are as solid as stone. They stand up to earthquakes, hurricanes, and tornadoes. Rammed-earth homes will not burn down in a fire. Fire hardens their outer walls and makes them even stronger. They also do not decay.

Like rammed earth, adobe bricks are made from mud, clay, and straw that is put into small molds. The sun-dried bricks are stacked. A mixture of mud and cement is used to attach the bricks together into walls.

Adobe can be recycled. If an adobe house is torn down, broken bricks can be mixed with mud to make new bricks. Unbroken bricks can be used to build a new building.

Adobe is a good thermal material. The heat from the sun stays inside adobe for a long time. This heat is then released into the house. Less energy is needed to create heat. This is a form of passive solar energy. Passive solar energy requires no machines or energy to gather it. Because no energy is used, no harm is done to the environment.

Straw-bale, rammed-earth, and adobe homes may be more Earth friendly than conventional houses, but they are not always easy to build. Few builders know how to properly use materials such as straw and adobe. And many communities will not allow houses to be made of these materials because less is known about them.

EARTHSHIPS

The name *Earthship* describes a kind of home built to function as its own little world, or Earth. It has special equipment to generate, or create, its own electricity. It includes solar panels that capture sunlight. The sunlight heats the house and shines on plants that are grown for food and to help keep the air clean.

An Earthship has a roof that catches snow and rain for use in the home. Giant containers store the melted snow and rainwater that water the plants and provide drinking, bathing, and cooking water.

An Earthship home is built from used materials that would have been thrown away—including old tires. Tires are made of a strong rubber. They can withstand the weight and force of a car driving fast along a street or highway. They last for many years. Water and other substances cannot leak through them.

Tires are so durable, in fact, that throwing them away creates a pollution problem. Inside a landfill or dump, tires break down

The tire walls of an Earthship are filled with rammed earth. Empty soda cans help fill the spaces between the tires.

This completed Earthship is in Taos, New Mexico.

into the soil very slowly. If the dump catches fire, tires burn for a long time and release dangerous toxins into the air.

As building blocks for an Earthship, however, tires can be an ideal material. They can be stacked together like bricks. Then they can be filled with dirt and covered with stucco or plaster.

Sometimes Earthships are built partway into the side of a hill. This allows the ground to act as insulation, keeping the home cool in the summer and warm in the winter.

GOING GREEN INSIDE

Your family might not be building or buying a new home. But existing houses can be made greener in many ways. They can be retrofitted, or renovated.

The actor Julia Louis-Dreyfus and her husband retrofitted their house in Southern California to make it greener. They added a roof that can be retracted, or pulled back, to let in sunlight and fresh air. It also pushes warm air out of the house without using electricity.

These changes cost a lot of money. But other options are available that cost much less and that many homeowners can make.

Solar water heaters can be installed in a home with an unshaded, south-facing roof. The heater uses the sun's energy to heat water for the home. No fossil fuels are used, and no pollutants are emitted into the air.

A house with a solar water heater may still need a gas or electric water heater. Depending on where the house is located, however, solar water heaters can heat up to 80 percent of the home's water.

Homeowners can replace many other appliances—such as dishwashers, refrigerators, washing machines, dryers, and air conditioners—with models that use less energy. They also can install thermostats that turn off heat and air-conditioning when they are not needed. New sensor switches even turn off lights when people leave the room. Fluorescent lighting uses less energy than incandescent lighting. This saves money on electric costs too.

The next time your home needs painting, you can use water-based, nontoxic paints. These are safer for the people and animals living in the home. Use brushes and rollers instead of sprayers so less paint is inhaled.

This solar heating system uses vacuum tubes to gather energy from the sun to heat water for the house.

Used carpet, light fixtures, and other building materials can be found at places like the ReUse Center. It is part of the Green Institute.

Another green option is to reuse materials instead of buying new ones. For example, the ReUse Center in Minnesota sells good-quality items from houses that were torn down. These items include kitchen cabinets, doors, windows, and wood for floors, panels, or decks. Homeowners might also find counters, tiles, bathtubs, sinks, toilets, carpet, and lights.

In the bathroom, homeowners can install low-flow showerheads and

ANNIE YOUNG

Garbage led Annie Young and other activists to create the Green Institute in Minneapolis. The city planned to build a garbage transfer station in Young's neighborhood. Young and other people met to think up ways to stop this.

One night Young had a dream. She dreamed of a glass building with solar panels and a wind machine. She and her friend built models of her "dream" building with Lego toys. Young used the models at meetings to show what her community wanted to build instead of the garbage transfer station.

The Green Institute that was finally built has pieces from Young's dream. It includes solar panels, large glass windows letting in sunlight, and a wetlands area.

low-flush toilets. These use less water. Old toilets flush 3 to 5 gallons (11 to 19 liters) of water and can use 40 percent of the water in a household. Low-flush and dual-flush toilets use 1.6 gallons (6 liters) or even less.

Outside your house, you can landscape with native plants. They often need much less water than nonnative flowers or grasses. They require little, if any, mowing or clipping. This means no lawn mowers are using electricity or gas. Native plants often do not require fertilizers to help them grow. Fertilizers can be toxic to the land, water, animals, and people living nearby.

LIVING ROOFTOPS

Some houses are green right up through the rooftop. Instead of tiles or shingles, gardens cover their roofs. Waterproof fabric is placed on a wooden frame. The frame holds dirt. Wildflowers and other plants grow out of the dirt.

Workers install a layer of a green roof on a city library. The green roof will capture rainwater and reuse it to water rooftop gardens.

MMUNITIES MAKING FFERENCE

Collections of things can be designed to help the environment as well. Houses can be grouped together using green ideas. Parks and gardens can support greener living for a whole neighborhood or town. Groups of people can create green ideas together and pass them into laws. These are all green communities—groups of people using green design in how they live, work, and play together.

COHOUSING COMMUNITIES

Cohousing is an idea that began in Denmark. Since then the idea has spread worldwide.

Cohousing clusters houses together into a community that shares things. Families have their own private homes, which are built around common houses and spaces. A common house might have one big room that everybody in the community can use. Kids can play together in the shared room. Space and building materials are saved because the houses do not each have a playroom.

Left: Many cohousing communities, such as EcoVillage at Ithaca (EVI), in New York, were designed to reduce people's impact on Earth. *Below:* The Greater World Earthship community is in Taos, New Mexico. All of the buildings collect power from the sun and water from the sky. They also heat and cool themselves passively.

Cohousing residents help cook dinner in the common house.

Every house in a cohousing community has its own kitchen. But the community might also share one big kitchen and dining room. Members take turns cooking a meal each night. Others who do not want to cook that night can meet in the big dining room and share the meal.

People in cohousing can share things they do not use all the time. Sharing things means fewer things are bought. This saves resources and reduces waste. People who like to build things can share their tools with others who seldom use tools. Children who want to try skiing can borrow other children's skis. Gardeners can come together to work in a large, shared garden.

People who live in cohousing units help make decisions about their community. They help decide how the units will be built. They decide how to manage their buildings. They decide who will do what tasks.

Sometimes, just as in families, people living in cohousing disagree or argue. They must find ways to get along. Learning this process helps people work and live together. Cohousing can help people learn skills that will help them all their lives.

Cohousing can be in the country or in the city. Many times, cohousing is near public transportation, such as bus lines. People can get places without driving. They can come home safely at night. They have a whole community of friends watching out for them.

CITY GARDENS

Community gardens can bring people together and improve buildings and neighborhoods. In Queens, New York, a huge new public garden has been built. The garden is on land that had been used as a dumping ground. The garden is helping to improve this land.

Queens Botanical Garden, in New York, features this LEED-certified building. Water that runs off its roof is reused in toilets and fountains.

These girls volunteered to work in a community garden in Beardstown, Illinois.

A green roof over part of one building is covered with plants native to the area. They insulate the inside of the building from outside noise. Rainwater feeds the plants on the roof. Another part of the roof catches rainwater and lets it flow into a pool. From there, the water flows into planted areas throughout the garden. Deep wells tap into water used for heating and cooling the gardens.

SEEDBALLS

You can start a healthy ecosystem in your own yard. How? Try making seedballs. Seedballs are made of clay and soil mixed with seeds and rolled into small balls. It's best to use the seeds of plants that can live well together, are native to the area, and will help the land. Toss the balls into bare spots in your yard. Rain will help the seeds sprout. The clay and soil then provide the young sprouts with nutrients. Use the recipe at http://www.pathtofreedom.com/pathproject/gardening/seedballs.shtml.

City Slicker Farms in Oakland, California, is a large community garden. It is in a poor area with few grocery stores that sell healthy foods. People who live in the neighborhood grow healthy foods in the garden. They set up market stands on Saturdays to buy and sell the foods. The neighbors learn—and teach one another—about gardening, cooking, and other activities that are healthy for people and for the land.

In Israel a group of people transformed unused land into a community garden called Bustan Brody. Group members persuaded leaders to visit and help raise funds. They drew attention to their project by building it on holidays. For example, they held a cleanup day on Tu B'Av, the Day of Love. They planted saplings on Tu B'Shvat, a Jewish holiday often celebrated with the planting of trees.

A GREEN TOWN IN KANSAS

The town of Hesston, Kansas, is a wildlife habitat. Wildlife habitats restore plants and animal life that have been threatened by construction. To be called a wildlife habitat, an area needs to provide food, water, and shelter for wildlife.

Hesston's Dyck arboretum, or tree garden, holds 18 acres (7 hectares) of plants native to the region. Native Kansas plants grow in front of the police station, pharmacy, and coffee shop. Many people's yards also grow native plants.

The garden is almost 4 square miles (10 sq. km). It has an irrigation system for watering plants. It hosts talks and other events. It has a place for composting garbage and spaces for dogs to run.

IT TAKES A VILLAGE

When people work together, they can go beyond a few streets. They can create green neighborhoods or even whole towns.

Around the United States, many neighborhoods are getting greener—or already have gone green. They have parks, green spaces, and gathering spaces. Many have farmers' markets and

The Dyck Arboretum sponsors native plantings at schools through the Earth Partnership for Schools program. These kids plant native plants at their school in nearby Witchita, Kansas.

German architect Rolf Disch stands on the rooftop of a community center in Freiburg, Germany. Disch designed the building to operate on renewable energy, such as solar power.

community gardens. Many offer alternative energy programs and green buildings.

In Freiburg, Germany, the whole community of Vauban is green. In the mid-1990s, people worked together to create the district. A public transport system connects houses and buildings. This allows people to travel easily without driving cars. Many do not even own cars. Families share a car instead.

Bike paths thread throughout the district. Schools, businesses, and shopping areas are within walking distance. Cars are not allowed in the central section of Vauban. So children can play safely and neighbors can meet and talk.

Sometimes people dream even bigger. One group of people wants to buy a whole island to devote to green living. Many of the people are vegans. They do not eat or use any animal products, such as meat or dairy. Everyone who lives together on the island will live by green principles.

GLOBAL COMMUNITIES

Another kind of green design community is making an impact on our planet's health. It is invisible but real. This community is made up of the ideas and actions

SHOPPING COMMUNITIES

If people stop buying things they do not need, they can help reduce waste and pollution. They would drive less and throw away less packaging.

In 2003 a group of friends agreed not to go shopping for one whole year. They bought only the things they really needed, such as toilet paper, food, and toothpaste. The community grew to include millions of members all over the world. The group started a website, http://www.freecycle.org. Through this website, people can trade things they don't want or find things they need.

of lawmakers, business leaders, and other people working together.

Some of these actions come from legislators who write, vote, and pass bills into law. Other actions come from people who contact their representative about issues. Sometimes a businessperson has an idea and works with others to implement it.

In California many new laws are greening the state. For example, a 2006 measure requires builders to offer solar-energy tiles as a roofing option. The bill helps people pay the cost of installing solar roofs.

In Boulder, Colorado, people voted for the world's first carbon tax in 2006. The tax adds about sixteen dollars per year to each homeowner's electric bill. Each business pays about forty-six dollars more. The extra money helps pay for a new climate action plan in Colorado. The plan's goal is to lower carbon levels in the air by 24 percent.

Some large cities, such as Singapore and London, have introduced

This sign in London tells drivers that they are about to enter a congestion charging zone.

congestion charging, or pricing, to restrict driving in certain parts of the city. Drivers must pay a fee to enter the main business districts during the busiest times of the day. People who live and work in these areas have noticed fewer accidents and cleaner air. More people have started biking or using public transportation. In London the money from the fees goes toward improving the city's public transportation system.

CHAPTER SIX

A GREENER FUTURE

Engineers, carmakers, architects, computer manufacturers, businesspeople, community leaders, mothers and fathers, teachers, and other people are exploring new ideas in green design. Some ideas are already being tested and used. Others are still being discussed.

DOWN THE ROAD WITH GREENER VEHICLES

About 467,000 hybrid cars were sold in the United States in 2006. Experts expect sales of hybrids to surpass sales of SUVs and luxury cars by 2011.

Car companies are building new kinds of diesel and hybrid cars. One new system by Mercedes-Benz shoots urea—a chemical found in urine—into the vehicle's exhaust. Urea helps reduce emissions of nitrogen oxides, which add to smog.

Some carmakers are working with fast-food restaurants. These places dispose of huge amounts of used cooking oil from their deep-fat fryers. Together, these businesses are developing ways to convert that wasted oil into fuel.

General Motors is designing a new car that runs on electricity. Lithium ion batteries start up GM's new car, called the Chevy Volt. An engine that runs on a very small amount of gas creates more electricity to keep the battery charged. Every day, the owner plugs the car into an ordinary electric socket to recharge the batteries. The Volt also uses a hydrogen fuel cell and ethanol-based gas.

Other possible energy sources would use no gas at all. Hydrogen, mixed with oxygen in fuel cells, could create the electricity needed to run a car.

Bottom: A fuel-cell sport-utility vehicle parks at a hydrogen gas station in Berlin, Germany. *Background image:* A woman uses recycled cooking oil to fill the tank of her car. The car has been specially designed to run on either vegetable oil or diesel fuel.

A race car with a solar-collecting surface speeds along using energy from the sun.

Hydrogen is a very clean fuel. In a stunt to show how clean it is, the mayor of Chicago, Richard M. Daley, drank the exhaust from a prototype, or model, of a hydrogen-powered car.

A nitrogen-powered car is another possibility. Liquid nitrogen can provide a lot of energy, and its use creates no pollution. But liquid nitrogen is expensive to store and move safely.

Solar power might someday drive cars. But it's not practical to put solar panels on the roof of a car. If the car is parked under a tree or inside a garage, the sun will not shine on the car, and it won't get power. Drivers, however, can recharge their cars from cells that gather and hold electricity created from the sun. Solar stations already have been built in cities such as Santa Monica and San Diego, California. One solar charger even powers a new Ferris wheel on Santa Monica Pier.

Companies have dreamed up other ideas that might never become reality. But the ideas are a start. They might help people create cars that do not hurt Earth—and that someday might even help heal it.

An annual contest in Los Angeles asks for new green car design ideas. One idea, the BioMoke car, would use biodegradable panels filled with seeds from palm trees. After the car was no longer used, the panels would biodegrade. The seeds would sprout into new plants.

Mercedes-Benz came up with an idea for a car made of 100 percent recyclable materials. Another entry, an Acura car, would be built with lightweight, recyclable materials and would be powered with a hydrogen fuel cell. The Hummer O2 Concept had panels filled with live algae. The algae would turn carbon dioxide into oxygen, just as trees do.

The design of the Toyota Renewable Lifestyle Vehicle (RLV) called for two seats, one behind the other—much like a bicycle built for two. Pedals pushed by the driver would recharge the battery and help supply power. The floorboard would be made of bamboo and aluminum.

The design for the Toyota Renewable Lifestyle Vehicle (RLV) shows how a vehicle can be part of a healthy lifestyle.

ELECTRONICS AND OTHER THINGS

Many computer and electronic companies are working with customers to reduce the amount of waste and pollution their products create. Dell, Hewlett-Packard, Apple, and Gateway offer take-back programs. People can return used computers to the companies that made them, instead of throwing them away. Sometimes the companies will even give people a small rebate on a new computer. That means the company will pay back part of the cost of the new computer.

These companies tear down the computers that they take back. They take out the plastic, glass, steel, and aluminum inside for reuse. They remove dangerous substances, such as cadmium, so that they do not go into landfills and poison the planet. They also remove gold, silver, palladium, and other precious metals.

Manufacturers also work with other companies and nonprofit groups to find places to send used computers that have been refurbished. (A refurbished computer has been restored to its earlier condition.) They send these computers to at-risk students, people with disabilities, and other groups who need computers.

Two workers carry newly packaged computers that were refurbished at an electronic products recycling center in China.

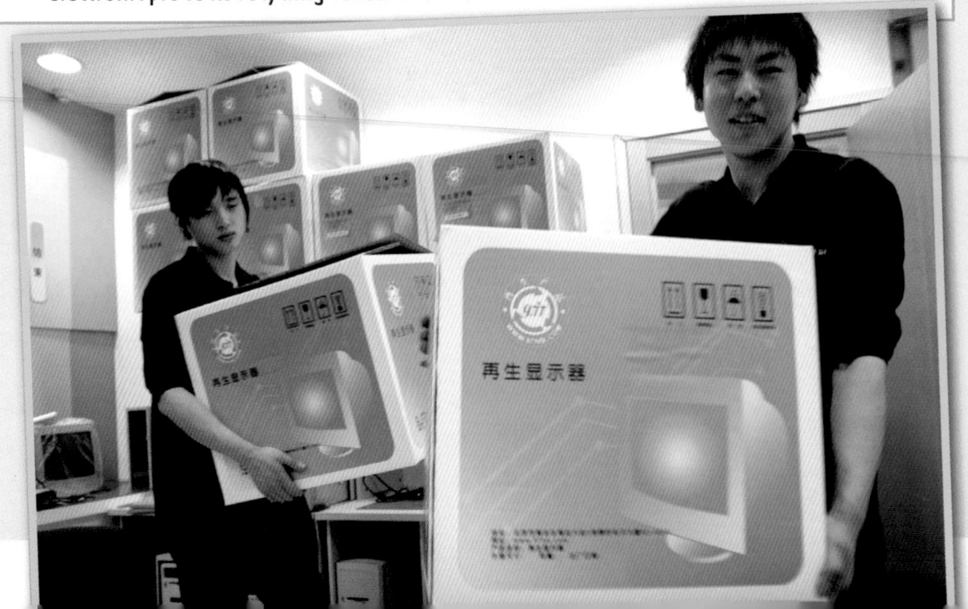

Nonelectronic things, such as clothing, are getting greener too. Old-fashioned cotton farming uses pesticides that poison the land, water, and air. Cotton farms take up large tracts of land that could be used for growing healthier things. Organic cotton farming uses no pesticides and less water.

More companies have begun offering clothing made from organic cotton because their customers have begun to demand it. Patagonia, Timberland, Levi's, the Gap, and Nike use at least some organic cotton in their products.

GREENER HOUSES AND BUILDINGS

After World War II (1939–1945), many soldiers returned home and were ready to start families. A building boom occurred in the United States. To meet the high demand for homes that did not cost much money, many prefab homes were built. *Prefab* is short for *prefabricated.* The one-size-fits-all parts come from a factory. A similar concept is called modular design.

New Earth-friendly houses are turning back to this old notion. Prefab or modular building design can save lumber and other materials. Modular designs use

A crane places a wall on a modular home.

WHY IS MODULAR EASIER?

Imagine that you have two carrots that are 6 inches (15 centimeters) long. Your dad asks you to cut them into six slices for dinner. He wants one slice to be 2.5 inches (6.4 cm) long and all the others to be 2 inches (5 cm) long.

You could cut three 2-inch slices from one carrot. But the other carrot would end up with one slice that was only 1.5 inches (3.8 cm) long. You would have to find another carrot to cut the final 2-inch slice.

But if your dad asked that all slices be the same length—2 inches—you could cut exactly six slices and have none left over. Plus, you could pile the carrots and cut through both at once.

Cutting lumber for houses works the same way. If lumber companies cut wood to a standard length and architects designed houses calling for lumber that is long, there would be less waste in building and the work could go faster.

modules, or parts, that are the same size, can be made at the same time, and can be interchanged. Because they fit many uses, they do not have to be trimmed to fit special sizes. No trimming means no wasted pieces, so modular houses cost less to build—and can be good for the planet.

New green building design also considers the placement and shape of a building. Putting a building at a different angle on the land can increase the amount of sun that warms the building.

These and other steps, such as planning where to grow trees and plants, increase the amount of passive and active solar energy the building absorbs. Taking advantage of passive solar energy can save 10 to 15 percent of the energy used for heating or cooling the house.

Solar and wind energy are fast-growing pieces in the green design picture. Many companies already sell rooftop windmills. These machines harness the

Bamboo floors look like regular wood floors. Most bamboo is grown in Asia.

wind and sometimes draw power from the sun. They allow homeowners to generate their own electricity. Further into the future, a home might become a mini power station of its own. The home would give energy back to the utility company instead of taking it.

New homes feature more renewable materials, such as bamboo, for floor coverings. The materials in the kitchen cabinets of Earth-friendly homes will not contain toxic chemicals, such as formaldehyde.

People are always coming up with new building concepts. For example, builders might plant house farms. These would have biological materials that grow into solid, thick forms, like living walls. The materials would include genes from strong trees, such as aspen or birch.

Panels could be cut from the walls, similar to how squares of turf are cut for lawns. These panels could be moved to the building site and attached to other panels. They would not require as much energy to move as large amounts of lumber and other old building materials. This would reduce the amount of pollutants emitted into the air.

Once at the building site, these panels would be watered with runoff water that otherwise would be wasted. The living walls would continue to grow into the final structure used to build the house.

BUILDING TOGETHER

One of the most important developments in green building is the idea of collaborating, or working together. When people collaborate, everyone involved in making and using a building talk over ideas together before beginning the work. These include contractors, architects, engineers, designers, material suppliers, and perhaps even the people who will live or work in the building.

In the past, this didn't happen, so the person designing the building did things that made it less energy efficient for the person using the building. Or the person building the house added things that weren't needed because of how it had been designed.

People stand in line to tour a modular home in New Orleans, Louisiana. The home was built in only nine weeks. Modular homes helped people in New Orleans replace houses destroyed by Hurricane Katrina in 2005.

For example, an engineer might have installed a big air-conditioning system that used a lot of energy. But if she had known that the builder planned to use high-quality windows with good insulation, she would have installed a smaller air-conditioning system that used less energy.

GREEN SCHOOLS

Many colleges and universities offer new programs to teach green design ideas. In 2006 Yale created the first biophilia master's degree program. *Biophilia* means that people are drawn to nature.

Biophilia students at Yale study architecture, forestry, and ecology. Architecture is the design of buildings. Forestry is the study of trees and forests. Ecology is the study of relationships in nature—for example, how plants interact with the water, soil, and animals in the same area.

The Adam Joseph Lewis Center for Environmental Studies at Oberlin College in Ohio is in a building surrounded by organic gardens, orchards, and wetlands. Much of it was built from biodegradable, recycled, or renewable materials. Its ongoing use of energy can be viewed on screens in the building.

In Rio de Janeiro, Brazil, one school has a class project called the Design Incubator. Students there created a way to turn resin from palm trees into a substance strong enough to use instead of wood.

People at these and many other schools are already finding new ways to make our planet healthier using green design. In the future, students like you will help Earth-friendly design flourish and grow throughout the twenty-first century.

Try these tips to help you live, travel, study, and shop more gently on our planet.

- **Reduce use of energy-consuming devices at home.** Turn off lights, TVs, and computers when not using them. Turn down the thermostat by 10°F (6°C) for eight hours during the night. This can save 5 to 10 percent on heating costs. Close curtains at night. Set the refrigerator between 35°F (1°C) and 38°F (3°C) and the freezer at 0°F (-18°C). Wash full loads in the washing machine. Use cold water and a high spin cycle. Dry your clothes on a drying rack or clothesline instead of in the dryer. Include native plants in your outdoor landscaping. Mow the lawn with a reel mower instead of a gas-powered mower.

- **Reduce waste when you travel.** Reduce your family's use of motorized vehicles. Ride your bike to school, or carpool with other families. Take the bus or walk when you can. Don't store heavy items in the car. A heavier vehicle will use more gas. Ask your parents to turn off the car, rather than letting it idle, if they are waiting for more than one minute. Remind your parents to keep the car's tires properly inflated. This will help improve the car's fuel economy.

- **Spread the word at school.** Show others by your actions how to reduce waste, save energy, and avoid health hazards. Pack your lunch in a box, bag, or container that you can reuse. Sort, recycle, or compost cafeteria trash. Encourage classmates and teachers to reuse or recycle paper. Turn off computers when not in use and at the end of the school day. Find out

Bring reusable bags to the grocery store to pack home your items.

what your school does with old computers. If your school bus uses diesel fuel, ask the driver to open bus windows so diesel exhaust fumes won't build up inside.

- **Take green steps at the store.** When you buy a small item, tell the clerk to keep the bag for the next customer. Carry your item in your pocket. Buy products with less packaging or that come in returnable, reusable, or recyclable containers. Use durable goods instead of disposable ones. Borrow books, DVDs, and other items from the library when you can instead of buying them new from a store. Buy recycled paper that was made without chlorine bleach. Use candles that have oil-free wax. Buy bamboo! Bamboo is easily renewable and can be grown without pesticides.

HOW TO WRITE TO YOUR LEGISLATOR

Write to your U.S. senators or representatives. Ask them to help pass laws that support green design. You can also write to companies that make things that you buy and use every day. Ask them to design and sell greener products.

You can send letters or e-mails. Some environmental groups can provide letters or petitions that you can copy and sign. However, a note that you write yourself will carry more weight than a form letter. Here are tips for writing to your legislators or to heads of companies:

- **Tell them how you feel about the topic.** Use your own words. Explain how a certain law or business practice would affect you, your family and friends, your school, or your community. Use facts, not opinions, to state your case.

- **Keep your letter short,** and describe only one issue. Identify a bill by its number and title if you can.

- **Ask for a reply** from the person to find out what he, she, or that company is doing to help the environment.

- **Write a thank-you note** if your legislator votes for or helps to pass a bill that you agree with. This will help the person remember you the next time you write.

- **Find postal and e-mail addresses** for U.S. senators at http://www.senate.gov and for representatives at http://www.house.gov. To contact a company, visit its website and click on "Contact Us."

y environmental organizations can provide more information about h-friendly design and how to help the planet. Here are just a few:

BuildingGreen, Inc.
http://www.buildinggreen.com
22 Birge St., Ste. 30
Brattleboro, VT 05301
802-257-7300

Natural Resources Defense Council
http://www.nrdc.org
40 W. 20th St.
New York, NY 10011
212-727-2700

Sierra Student Coalition
http://www.ssc.org/
600 14th St. NW, Ste. 750
Washington, DC 20005
-888-JOIN-SSC

Young Environmentalist Actions (YEA)
Global Response
http://www.globalresponse.org/kidsactions.php
P.O. Box 7490
Boulder, CO 80306
303-444-0306

GLOSSARY

active solar energy: energy from the sun that is captured with the aid of a device that often uses electrical or other energy sources to boost the amount of solar energy gathered

architecture: the design of buildings

atmosphere: the layer of gasses that surrounds Earth

biodegrade: to break down, or decay

biofuel: a fuel that is made from organic material rather than from nonrenewable fuels

carbon monoxide: a colorless, odorless, poisonous gas, produced by incomplete burning of carbon-based fuels, including gasoline, oil, and wood

cohousing: a form of housing that clusters homes together into a community that shares things

collaborate: to work together with other people

ecology: the study of relationships in nature—for example, how plants interact with the water, soil, and animals in the same area

ecosystem: a community of living things that depend on one another and their shared environment

forestry: the study of trees and forests

fossil fuel: a nonrenewable form of fuel that is created from the fossilized remains of buried life-forms and is dug from the ground. Oil, natural gas, and coal are fossil fuels.

global warming: the warming of Earth because of increased carbon dioxide and other heat-trapping gases in the atmosphere

green design: a way of designing, building, and using items that reduces or eliminates environmental harm to the planet. This is also called Earth friendly, sustainable, or eco-design.

life cycle: all phases involved in the design, manufacture, marketing, use, reuse, and disposal of a building, car, or product

modular: consisting of parts that are the same size, can be made at the same time, and can be interchanged

passive solar energy: energy from the sun that is captured without any external power sources, by using, for example, the design of a building to maximize sunlight

pollutant: a substance that makes the land, air, or water dirty

sustainable: practiced or used in a way that doesn't destroy or permanently damage a resource

SOURCE NOTE

40 Annie Young, Green Institute, Minneapolis, e-mail interview with the author, November 28, 2006, and December 3, 2006.

SELECTED BIBLIOGRAPHY

Carnegie Mellon. *Green Design Institute.* N.d. http://www.ce.cmu.edu/GreenDesign/ (February 18, 2008).

Center for Energy Efficiency and Renewable Technologies. *Clean Power Campaign.* February 18, 2008. http://www.cleanpower.org (February 18, 2008).

Chiras, Daniel D. *The Natural House: A Complete Guide to Healthy, Energy-Efficient, Environmental Homes.* White River Junction, VT: Chelsea Green Publishing, 2000.

EcoHousing Corporation. 2007. http://www.ecohousing.net/ (February 18, 2008).

Environmental Action. 2008. http://www.environmental-action.org/ (February 18, 2008).

Environmental Defense. 2007. http://www.environmentaldefense.org/ (February 18, 2008).

Green Institute. 2007. http://www.greeninstitute.org/ (February 18, 2008).

NBM. "The Green House." *National Building Museum.* http://www.nbm.org/Exhibits/greenHouse2/greenHouse.htm (February 18, 2008).

Snell, Clarke. *The Good House Book: A Common-Sense Guide to Alternative Homebuilding.* New York: Lark Books, 2004.

Tree Media Group. *Global Green USA.* 2006. http://www.globalgreen.org/ (February 18, 2008).

U.S. Environmental Protection Agency and U.S. Department of Energy. *Energy Star.* 2008. http://www.energystar.gov/ (February 18, 2008).

U.S. Green Building Council. 2008. http://www.usgbc.org (February 18, 2008).

JRTHER READING

gy Star
http://www.energystar.gov
The Energy Star site offers lots of information about ways to save energy. Sections focus on products, home improvement, buildings and plants, and new homes.

ll, Ron. *Earth-Friendly Energy.* Minneapolis: Lerner Publications Company, 2009. Find out about alternative sources of energy that could help save our planet.

Economy
http://www.fueleconomy.gov
This site has an online tool that compares and contrasts new and used cars for mileage, greenhouse gas emissions, safety, and more. Learn about hybrids and alternative fuel vehicles, or measure your family car's "energy impact" score.

al Green USA
http://www.globalgreen.org
Global Green focuses on Earth-friendly building in cities and schools, clean water, recycling, and more.

's Green Squad
http://www.nrdc.org/greensquad
This site from the Natural Resources Defense Council describes what actions you can take to make your school a greener, healthier place.

x, Charlotte. *Earth-Friendly Waste Management.* Minneapolis: Lerner Publications Company, 2009. Learn more about environmental problems caused by waste and ways of managing, recycling, and reducing waste to help save our planet.

/Center for a New American Dream
http://www.ibuydifferent.org/
Find out how changing the way you live and what you buy can make a difference to the environment.

INDEX

ABOUT THE AUTHOR

Anne Welsbacher has written about wading birds, pelicans, and the Hawaiian rain forest for Lerner Publications Company. She has written other books on animals, physical sciences, and the states. She has lived in Minnesota, California, and Kansas. She enjoys the animals and plants that live in all those states—especially in the tall grasses of Kansas.

PHOTO ACKNOWLEDGMENTS

The images in this book are used with the permission of © Patrick Lin/Getty Images, pp. 1, 3 (top); © Peter Menzel/drr.net, p. 3 (bottom); © iStockphoto.com/Daniel Stein, p. 4; Photo Courtesy of NASA, p. 4; © H. Armstrong Roberts/ClassicStock/The Image Works, p. 6; © Deserttrends/Dreamstime.com, p. 7; istockphoto.com/Midhat Becar, p. 8; John W. Warden/Stock Connection/Rex Features USA, p. 8; © Todd Strand/Independent Picture Service, pp. 9, 19, 41, 47, 54, 58, 63; © Jim West/Alamy, p. 11; © Photodisc/Getty Images, pp. 13, 23; istockphoto.com/ Sandy Jones, p. 14; © Julie Caruso/Independent Picture Service, p. 15; webking/Dreamstime.com, p. 16; Rex Features USA, p. 17; © Nigel Cattlin/ Visuals Unlimited, p. 18; © moodboard/fotolia, p. 20; © iStockphoto.com/Owen Price, p. 21; © Julie Caruso, p. 24; © Tomboy2290/Dreamstime.com, p. 25; © Joanne Ciccarello/ Christian Science Monitor/Getty Images, p. 26; © Gehringj/Dreamstime.com, p. 27; AP Photo/The Plian Dealer, Lynn Ischay, p. 28; © Mark Boulton/Alamy, p. 29; © iStockphoto .com/Charles Silvey, p. 31; © Jeff Morgan alternative energy/Alamy, pp. 32, 35; © Allan Baxter/Photographer's Choice/Getty Images, p. 33; © Luchschen/Dreamstime.com, p. 34; © Kevin Judd/Cephas Picture Library/Alamy, p. 36; © Alix Henry, pp. 37, 43; AP Photo/ Eric Draper, p. 38; © Duncan Hale-Sutton/Alamy, p. 39; Courtesy of the Green Institute, p. 40; © Kone/Dreamstime.com, p. 41; © Robert Nickelsberg/Getty Images, pp. 42, 44; © Jeff Goldberg/Esto, p. 45; © Journal-Courier/Steve Warmowski/The Image Works, p. 46; © Courtesy of Dyck Arboretum, p. 48; AP Photo/Winfried Rothermel, p. 49; © Stillfx/ Dreamstime.com, p. 50; © Alan Copson/Alamy, p. 51; © Robyn Beck/AFP/Getty Images, p. 53 (background); AP Photo/Michael Sohn, p. 53 (inset); © Toyota RLV Designer: Kevin J. Chun and Calty Design Research, Inc., p. 55; UPPA/Photoshot, p. 56; © altrendo images/ Getty Images, p. 57; © Maxfx/Dreamstime.com, p. 59; © Mario Tama/Getty Images, p. 60.

Front cover: © Tim Boyle/Getty Images (top left); AP Photo/Eric Draper (bottom right); © Patrick Lin/Getty Images (top right); istockphoto.com/Mark Stay (background).